CHARLES TOMLINSON

The Way In

and Other Poems

LONDON
OXFORD UNIVERSITY PRESS
NEW YORK   TORONTO
1974

Oxford University Press, Ely House, London W.1

GLASGOW NEW YORK TORONTO MELBOURNE WELLINGTON
CAPE TOWN IBADAN NAIROBI DAR ES SALAAM LUSAKA ADDIS ABABA
DELHI BOMBAY CALCUTTA MADRAS KARACHI LAHORE DACCA
KUALA LUMPUR SINGAPORE HONG KONG TOKYO

ISBN 0 19 211842 0

© *Oxford University Press 1974*

PRINTED IN GREAT BRITAIN
BY THE BOWERING PRESS LIMITED, PLYMOUTH

FOR
BRENDA

CONTENTS

vii

ACKNOWLEDGMENTS

Acknowledgements are due to the editors of the following periodicals in which some of these poems first appeared :
Agenda, The Christian Science Monitor, The Critical Quarterly, The Hudson Review, The Listener, London Magazine, New Poetry (Australia), *Plural* (Mexico City), *Poetry Nation, Stand, The Times Literary Supplement.* I must also thank the producer of the B.B.C. 'Poetry Now' programme.

I MANSCAPES

THE WAY IN

The needle-point's swaying reminder
    Teeters at thirty, and the flexed foot
Keeps it there. Kerb-side signs
    For demolitions and new detours,
A propped pub, a corner lopped, all
    Bridle the pressures that guide the needle.

I thought I knew this place, this face
    A little worn, a little homely.
But the look that shadows softened
    And the light could grace, keeps flowing away from me
In daily change; its features, rendered down,
    Collapse expressionless, and the entire town

Sways in the fume of the pyre. Even the new
    And mannerless high risers tilt and wobble
Behind the deformations of acrid heat—
    A century's lath and rafters. Bulldozers
Gobble a street up, but already a future seethes
    As if it had waited in the crevices :

A race in transit, a nomad hierarchy :
    Cargoes of debris out of these ruins fill
Their buckled prams; their trucks and hand-carts wait
    To claim the dismantlings of a neighbourhood—
All that a grimy care from wastage gleans,
    From scrap-iron down to heaps of magazines.

Slowing, I see the faces of a pair
    Behind their load : he shoves and she
Trails after him, a sexagenarian Eve,
    Their punishment to number every hair
Of what remains. Their clothes come of their trade—
    They wear the cast-offs of a lost decade.

The place had failed them anyhow, and their pale
    Absorption staring past this time
And dusty space we occupy together,
    Gazes the new blocks down—not built for them;
But what they are looking at they do not see.
    No Eve, but mindless Mnemosyne,

3

She is our lady of the nameless metals, of things
    No hand has made, and no machine
Has cut to a nicety that takes the mark
    Of clean intention—at best, the guardian
Of all that our daily contact stales and fades,
    Rusty cages and lampless lampshades.

Perhaps those who have climbed into their towers
    Will eye it all differently, the city spread
In unforeseen configurations, and living with this,
    Will find that civility I can only miss—and yet
It will need more than talk and trees
    To coax a style from these disparities.

The needle-point's swaying reminder
    Teeters : I go with uncongealing traffic now
Out onto the cantilevered road, window on window
    Sucked backwards at the level of my wheels.
Is it patience or anger most renders the will keen?
    This is a daily discontent. This is the way in.

NIGHT RIDE

The lamps are on : terrestrial galaxies,
    Fixed stars and moving. How many lights,
How many lives there are, cramped in beside
    This swathe of roadway. And its sodium circuits
Have ousted the glimmer of a thousand hearths
    To the margins of estates whose windows
Blaze over pastoral parentheses. Scatterings
    Trace out the contours of heights unseen,
Drip pendants across their slopes.
    Too many of us are edging behind each other
With dipped beams down the shining wet.
    Our lights seem more beautiful than our lives
In the pulse and grip of this city with neither
    Time nor space in which to define
Itself, its style, as each one feels
    His way among the catseyes and glittering asterisks
And home on home reverberates our wheels.

4

AT STOKE

I have lived in a single landscape. Every tone
   And turn have had for their ground
These beginnings in grey-black : a land
   Too handled to be primary—all the same,
The first in feeling. I thought it once
   Too desolate, diminished and too tame
To be the foundation for anything. It straggles
   A haggard valley and lets through
Discouraged greennesses, lights from a pond or two.
   By ash-tips, or where the streets give out
In cindery in-betweens, the hills
   Swell up and free of it to where, behind
The whole vapoury, patched battlefield,
   The cows stand steaming in an acrid wind.
This place, the first to seize on my heart and eye,
   Has been their hornbook and their history.

HOKUSAI ON THE TRENT

This milky sky of a dragging afternoon
   Seems a painter's sky—the vision of a lack,
A thwarted possibility that broods
   On the meanness and exclusion. This could well be
An afternoon sunk in eternity
   But for the traffic tolling the rush hour
Among blackened houses, back to back
   And the tang of the air (its milk is sour) :
And what painting could taste of such dragging afternoons
   Whose tints are tainted, whose Fujiyamas slag ?

ETRURIA VALE

Nineteen-thirty, our window had for view
The biggest gasometer in England.
Time, no doubt, has robbed that record, too.
The waste ground disappeared beneath the houses.
Faced with the scale of all this, I'm as lost
As if I were Josiah Wedgwood's ghost
Compelled to follow out the tow-path through
The place he named Etruria. In the darkness
He might still bark his shins against the rungs
His barges moored beside. His sooted house
Flares nightly in the gusty lightnings as
The foundries pour their steel. The plan had been
A factory and model cottages,
A seat and prospect for a gentleman,
But history blackened round him, time drank up
The clear wine of his intention, left the lees
Staining the bottom of the valley's cup.
The gas tank has the air of an antique.
And nineteen-thirty was another century.

GLADSTONE STREET

It was the place to go in nineteen-thirty,
And so we went. A housemaid or two
Still lingered on at the bigger houses.
A miner and his family were the next
To follow us there, had scarcely settled in
When the wife began dying, whitely visible
Through the bay window in their double bed.
At the back, the garden vanished
Under grass and a ramshackle shed.
People were sure the street was going downhill.
It literally was : cracks in our hall
Opened as the house started to subside
Towards the mines beneath. Miners were everywhere

Under that cancerous hill. My mother swore
That you could hear them tapping away below
Of a quiet night. Miners unnerved her so
Ever since one sat beside her on the train
And soiled her with his pit dirt. But it wasn't miners
Undid the street. The housemaids lasted
Until the war, then fed the factories.
Flat-dwellers came and went, in the divided houses,
Mothers unwedded who couldn't pay their rent.
A race of gardeners died, and a generation
Hacked down the walls to park their cars
Where the flowers once were. It was there it showed,
The feeble-minded style of the neighbourhood
Gone gaudily mad in painted corrugations,
Botches of sad carpentry. The street front has scarcely changed.
No one has recorded the place.
Perhaps we shall become sociology. We have outpaced
Gladstone's century. We might have been novels.

DATES: PENKHULL NEW ROAD

It was new about eighteen-sixty.
Eighteen-sixty had come to stay, and did
Until the war—the second war, I mean.
Wasn't forty-five our nineteen-seventeen—
The revolution we had all of us earned?
Streamers and trestles in the roadway :
Even the climate rhymed with the occasion
And no drop fell. Eighteen-sixty
The architecture still insisted, gravely neat :
Alleyways between the houses, doors
That opened onto a still car-less street.
Doorsteps were once a civil place. There must have been a date
It came to be thought common and too late
In time, to be standing shouting out there
Across to the other side—the side
I envied, because its back-yards ran sheer
To the factory wall, warm, black, pulsating,

A long, comforting brick beast. I returned
In seventy-three. Like England,
The place had half-moved with the times—the 'other side'
Was gone. Something had bitten a gap
Out of the stretch we lived in. Penkhull still crowned
The hill, rebuilt to a plan—may as well scrap
The architectural calendar : that dream
Was dreamed up by the insurance-man
And we've a long time to live it yet.
The factory wore a half-bereaved, half-naked look . . .
It took time to convince me that I cared
For more than beauty : I write to rescue
What is no longer there—absurd
A place should be more fragile than a book.

PORTRAIT OF THE ARTIST I

One day, his mother took him on the tram.
An octogenarian in a mackintosh
Who still possessed the faculty for veneration,
Leaned across the aisle to her and said :
'That boy of yours has a remarkable forehead—
He'll live to be lord mayor.' He didn't rise
To that, but forehead letting instinct choose,
Betrayed him into verse. So Whittington
Never turned again, his mother strayed
Bemused between the prophecy and its failure.
The tram-lines were dragged up the very next year.

PORTRAIT OF THE ARTIST II

Season of mists and migraines, rich catarrhs,
Pipes in the public library throbbed and hissed
Against your advent. Parks were emptying.
Soaked benches and a wind that brought the grime

Smoking across the beds, now flowerless,
Drove old men indoors to the reading room.
They took their time, pored over magazines
They scarcely saw, and breathed-in dust and newsprint,
Clearing their throats to splatter on the floor.
Across the street, the high school lunch-hour raged.
He brought his sandwiches inside. Of course,
It was forbidden. The old illiterates, too,
Dragged orts and fragments from their paper bags.
A schoolboy and a dozen ancients, they
Watched for the librarian's bureaucracy
Who tried to spy them out, but seldom could—
They'd grown so adept at their secret feeding,
Bent at those tables others used for reading . . .
Did the old guilt stick? For now, he wrote
His verses furtively, on blotters, minutes,
As though back there, that surreptitious snack
Still hidden by *The Illustrated London News*.

THE TREE

This child, shovelling away
what remains of snow—
a batter of ash and crystals—
knows nothing of the pattern
his bent back lifts
above his own reflection :
it climbs the street-lamp's stem
and cross-bar, branching
to take in all the lines
from gutter, gable, slates
and chimney-crowns to the high
pillar of a mill chimney
on a colourless damp sky :
there in its topmost air
and eyrie rears that tree
his bending sends up
from a treeless street, its roots
in the eye and in the net the shining
flagstones spread at his feet.

9

MIDLANDS

Rain baptizes the ravaged counties
   In the name of some god who can remember
The way the land lay, the groundswell
   Under it all. The football club,
Treading back to mud their threadbare pitch,
   Move garish on the grey, hemmed-
In by a throng of sodden houses
   Whose Sunday kitchens grow savoury for them.

IN THE WARD

Old women come here to die. Nurses
   Tend them with a sort of callous zest
That keeps their youthful patience, guarantees it
   In face of all they do not wish to be :
Shrunk limbs, shrunk lives, the incontinence.
   A woodland scene is hanging on the wall,
To rectify some lost connection
   With a universe that goes on shepherding its flock
Of fogs out there, its unkillable seasons.
   Dying, these old have for an ally still
That world of repetitions for, once gone,
   They are replaced incessantly. In the ward
The picture-glass gives back the outlines
   Of both old and young, in a painted
Sunlight and among the twines of trees.

THE MARL PITS

It was a language of water, light and air
   I sought—to speak myself free of a world
Whose stoic lethargy seemed the one reply
   To horizons and to streets that blocked them back

In a monotone fume, a bloom of grey.
    I found my speech. The years return me
To tell of all that seasoned and imprisoned :
    I breathe familiar, sedimented air
From a landscape of disembowellings, underworlds
    Unearthed among the clay. Digging
The marl, they dug a second nature
    And water, seeping up to fill their pits,
Sheeted them to lakes that wink and shine
    Between tips and steeples, streets and waste
In slow reclaimings, shimmers, balancings,
    As if kindling Eden rescinded its own loss
And words and water came of the same source.

CLASS

Those midland *a*'s
once cost me a job :
diction defeated my best efforts—
I was secretary at the time
to the author of *The Craft of Fiction*.
That title was full of class.
You had only to open your mouth on it
to show where you were born
and where you belonged. I tried
time and again I tried
but I couldn't make it
that top *A—ah*
I should say—
it sounded like gargling.
I too visibly shredded his fineness :
it was clear the job couldn't last
and it didn't. Still, I'd always thought him an ass
which he pronounced arse. There's no accounting for taste.

THE RICH

I like the rich—the way
they say : 'I'm not made of money' :
their favourite pastoral
is to think they're not rich at all—
poorer, perhaps, than you or me,
for they have the imagination of that fall
into the pinched decency
we take for granted. Of course,
they do want to be wanted
by all the skivvies and scrapers
who neither inherited nor rose.
But are they daft or deft,
when they proclaim themselves
men of the left, as if prepared
at the first premonitory flush
of the red dawn
to go rushing onto the street
and, share by share,
add to the common conflagration
their scorned advantage?
They know that it can't happen
in Worthing or Wantage :
with so many safety valves
between themselves and scalding,
all they have to fear
is wives, children, breath and balding.
And at worst
there is always some sunny
Aegean prospect. I like the rich—
they so resemble the rest
of us, except for their money.

BRIDGES

The arteries, red lane on lane,
    Cover the engineers' new maps :
England lies lost to silence now :
    On bridges, where old roads cross

12

The chasm of the new, the idlers
　　Stand staring down. Philosophers
Of the common run, some masticate pipe-stems,
　　And seem not to hear the roar in Albion's veins,
As though the quiet, rebegotten as they lean, survived
　　Through them alone, its stewards and sustainers,
For all these advancing and disappearing lives.

AT SAINT MARY'S CHURCH

The high nave, in a place of ships,
　　Seems like the invitation to some voyage
Long deferred. It will not be undertaken now.
　　Saint Mary's shares a horizon
With blocks in a mock stone-brown
　　Meant to resemble hers. This cheek by jowl affair
Labours to prove we can equal or outdo
　　Those eras of cholera, fear of the mob.
If that is true, it is not true here.
　　Elizabeth thought this church the comeliest
She had seen, and haunts it still, solid
　　In painted wood, and carved by the same
Hands as those, that in a place of ships,
　　Shaped gaudy figure-heads. And though
That voyage is not to be undertaken, she,
　　All bright will, female insouciance,
Might well have been the thrust and prow
　　To such a venture now forsaken
In the dust of abolished streets, the land-
　　Locked angles of a stale geometry.
　　　　　　　　　　　　　　　　　　Bristol

IN A BROOKLYN PARK

'To people these lands with civil men',
　　George Jackson said. There is civility enough
Inside this place, if one could spread it :
　　A woman is trying to reconcile
Two fighting boys who still refuse
　　To smile with the bright persuasion of her smile;
An old man sits learning from a book
　　Inglés sin Maestro, while among the trees
Wander three generations of the Jews.

II UNDER THE MOON'S REIGN

UNDER THE MOON'S REIGN

Twilight was a going of the gods : the air
    Hung weightlessly now—its own
Inviolable sign. From habit, we
    Were looking still for what we could not see—
The inside of the outside, for some spirit flung
    From the burning of that Götterdämmerung
And suffused in the obscurity. Scraps
    Of the bare-twigged scene were floating
Scattered across scraps of water—mirrors
    Shivered and stuck into a landscape
That drifted visibly to darkness. The pools
    Restrained the disappearing shapes, as all around
The dusk was gaining : too many images
    Beckoned from that thronging shade
None of which belonged there. And then the moon
    Drawing all into more than daylight height
Had taken the zenith, the summit branches
    Caught as by steady lightning, and each sign
Transformed, but by no more miracle than the place
    It occupied and the eye that saw it
Gathered into the momentary perfection of the scene
    Under transfigured heavens, under the moon's reign.

FOXES' MOON

    Night over England's interrupted pastoral,
        And moonlight on the frigid lattices
Of pylons. The shapes of dusk
        Take on an edge, refined
By a drying wind and foxes bring
        Flint hearts and sharpened senses to
This desolation of grisaille in which the dew
        Grows clearer, colder. Foxes go
In their ravenous quiet to where
        The last farm meets the first

Row from the approaching town : they nose
    The garbage of the yards, move through
The white displacement of a daily view
    Uninterrupted. Warm sleepers turn,
Catch the thin volpine bark between
    Dream on dream, then lose it
To the babbling undertow they swim. These
    Are the fox hours, cleansed
Of all the meanings we can use
    And so refuse them. Foxes glow,
Ghosts unacknowledged in the moonlight
    Of the suburb, and like ghosts they flow
Back, racing the coming red, the beams
    Of early cars, a world not theirs
Gleaming from kindled windows, asphalt, wires.

THE DREAM

Under that benign calm eye that sees
    Nothing of the vista of land and sky
It brings to light; under the interminably
    Branching night, of street and city,
Vein and artery, a dream
    Held down his mind that blinded him
To all except the glimmering, closed-in warmth
    Of his own present being. Alone
And yet aware within that loneliness
    Of what he shared with others—a sense
Of scope and pleasure in mere warmth—
    He seemed the measure of some constricted hope
That asked a place in which it might pursue
    Its fulness, and so grew away from him,
Swayed into palpability like a wall :
    He knew that he must follow out its confine
To his freedom, and be taught this tense fluidity
    Always a thought beyond him. His hand
Still feeling for that flank of stone,
    The space that opened round him might have grown there
For the resurrection of a being buried

18

By the reality that too much defined it : now
The transitions of the dream, the steps and streets,
    The passageways that branched beneath
Haphazard accumulation of moon on moon,
    Spurned at each turn a reality
Merely given—an inert threat
    To be met with and accommodated. The ways
He walked seemed variants on a theme
    Shaped by a need that was greed no longer,
The dream of a city under the city's dream,
    Proportioned to the man whom sleep replenishes
To stand reading with opened eyes
    The intricacies of the imagined spaces there
Strange and familiar as the lines that map a hand.

AFTER A DEATH

A little ash, a painted rose, a name.
    A moonshell that the blinding sky
Puts out with winter blue, hangs
    Fragile at the edge of visibility. That space
Drawing the eye up to its sudden frontier
    Asks for a sense to read the whole
Reverted side of things. I wanted
    That height and prospect such as music brings—
Music or memory. Neither brought me here.
    This burial place straddles a green hill,
Chimneys and steeples plot the distances
    Spread vague below : only the sky
In its upper reaches keeps
    An untarnished January colour. Verse
Fronting that blaze, that blade,
    Turns to retrace the path of its dissatisfactions,
Thought coiled on thought, and only certain that
    Whatever can make bearable or bridge
The waste of air, a poem cannot.
    The husk of moon, risking the whole of space,
Seemingly sails it, frailly launched
    To its own death and fulness. We buried

A little ash. Time so broke you down,
    Your lost eyes, dry beneath
Their matted lashes, a painted rose
    Seems both to memorialize and mock
What you became. It picks your name out
    Written on the roll beside a verse—
Obstinate words : measured against the blue,
    They cannot conjure with the dead. Words,
Bringing that space to bear, that air
    Into each syllable we speak, bringing
An earnest to us of the portion
    We must inherit, what thought of that would give
The greater share of comfort, greater fear—
    To live forever, or to cease to live?
The imageless unnaming upper blue
    Defines a world, all images
Of endeavours uncompleted. Torn levels
    Of the land drop, street by street,
Pitted and pooled, its wounds
    Cleansed by a light, dealt out
With such impartiality you'd call it kindness,
    Blindly assuaging where assuagement goes unfelt.

III ELEMENTS

ELEMENTAL

A last flame,
sole leaf
flagging at the tree tip,
is dragged through the current
down into the water
of the air, and in this final
metamorphosis, spiralling
swims to earth.

IN DECEMBER

Cattle are crowding the salt-lick.
The gruel of mud icily thickens.
On the farm-boy's Honda a sweat of fog drops.
They are logging the woodland, the sole standing crop.

HYPHENS

'The country's love-
liness', it said :
what I read was
'the country's love-
lines'—the unnec-
essary 's'
passed over by
the mind's blind-
ly discriminating eye :
but what I saw
was a whole scene
restored : the love-

lines drawing
together the list
'loveliness' capped
and yet left
vague, unloved :
lawns, gardens, houses,
the encircling trees.

IN MARCH

These dry, bright winter days,
   When the crow's colour takes to itself
Such gloss, the shadows from the hedge
   Ink-stain half way across
The road to where a jagged blade
   Of light eats into them : light's guarded frontier
Is glittering everywhere, everywhere held
   Back by naked branchwork, dark
Fissurings along the creviced walls,
   Shade side of barn and house, of half-cut stack
Strawing the ground, in its own despite
   With flecks of pallid gold, allies to light :
And over it all, a chord of glowing black
   A shining, flying shadow, the crow is climbing.

DISCREPANCIES

That year, March began in April.
Wasn't its floes from Greenland
Going south, they said, and the earthquake
In Nicaragua—a collision between
The seismic and the atmospheric that released
An effervescence into the air ? Its tang and sting

Excited the nostrils of the yearling,
The dead leaves circling rose again
But the clouds said, 'Snow, snow',
The sun melting the threat before it fell.
Nicaragua blazed into the chaos,
A polar glittering of gulls
Swung round and round on the mid-air currents
Over the windswept bed of their inland sea.
Nature has evolved beyond us—
You couldn't have painted it, I mean,
Unless on the whirlpool's fish-eye mirror
Where the blinding navel winds all discrepancies in.

THE LAST OF NIGHT

Mist after frost. The woodlands
stretch vague in it, but catch
the rising light on reefs
of foliage above the greyish
'sea' I was about to say,
but sun so rapidly advances
between glance and word,
under that leafy headland
mist lies a sea no more :
a gauze visibly fading
burns out to nothing, lets grow
beneath each mid-field bush
a perfect shadow, and among
frost-whitened tussocks
the last of night recedes along
tracks the animals have taken
back into earth and wood.

THE WITNESSES

Now that the hillside woods are dense with summer,
    One enters with a new, an untaught sense
Of heights and distances. Before,
    Lacking the profusion, the protrusion of the leaves,
Spaces seemed far shallower that, now,
    Thronged with ledges of overhanging green,
Bear down on the air beneath. One can no longer see
    The high recession stretching beyond each tree,
But the view, shut round, lets through
    The mind into a palpitation of jostled surfaces.
Nudging, they overlap, reach out
    Beckoning, bridging the underdeeps that stir
Unsounded among the foliage of a hundred trees
    That fill an aerial city's every thoroughfare
With the steady vociferation of unhuman witnesses.

HILL WALK
for Philippe and Anne-Marie Jaccottet

Innumerable and unnameable, foreign flowers
    Of a reluctant April climbed the slopes
Beside us. Among them, rosemary and thyme
    Assuaged the coldness of the air, their fragrance
So intense, it seemed as if the thought
    Of that day's rarity had sharpened sense, as now
It sharpens memory. And yet such pungencies
    Are there an affair of every day—Provençal
Commonplaces, like the walls, recalling
    In their broken sinuousness, our own
Limestone barriers, half undone
    By time, and patched against its sure effacement
To retain the lineaments of a place.
    In our walk, time used us well that rhymed
With its own herbs. We crested idly
    That hill of ilexes and savours to emerge
Along the plateau at last whose granite

Gave on to air : it showed us then
The place we had started from and the day
   Half gone, measured against the distances
That lay beneath, a territory travelled.
   All stretched to the first fold
Of that unending landscape where we trace
   Through circuits, drops and terraces
The outworks, ruinous and overgrown,
   Where space on space has labyrinthed past time :
The unseizable citadel glimmering back at us,
   We contemplated no assault, no easy victory :
Fragility seemed sufficiency that day
   Where we sat by the abyss, and saw each hill
Crowned with its habitations and its crumbled stronghold
   In the scents of inconstant April, in its cold.

LACOSTE

De Sade's rent walls let in
   Through faceless windows, a sky
As colourless as the stones that framed them :
   All tenacity, a dry ivy grew
Bristling against the grey. But wild thyme
   Sweetened anew the memory of the spot,
Its scent as fresh as a single fig-tree's
   Piercing greenness. The only words
I heard in that place were kind ones—
   'If you would care to visit my house . . .'
—And came from the old woman who
   Paused in climbing the broken street
At meeting us : but we were *en voyage*
   So she, wishing us a good one, bent on
Once more against the devious, sloped track,
   We winding down a descent that led
Back to the valley vineyards' spread geometry.

27

HOW FAR

How far from us
even the nearest are
among these close leaves
crowding the window :

what we know
of that slow then sudden
bursting into green is merely
what we have seen of it and not

(fermenting at its heart)
darkness such as the blind might hear :
for us, there is no way in where
across these surfaces

the light is a white lie
told only to hide the dark
extent from us
of a seafloor continent.

TIGER SKULL

Frozen in a grimace, all cavernous threat,
onslaught remains its sole end still :
handle it, and you are taught the weight
such a thrust to kill would carry.

The mind too eagerly marries a half truth. This carapace
lies emptied of the memory of its own sated peace,
its bestial repose and untensed pride
under the equanimity of sun and leaf,

where to be tiger is
to move through the uncertain terrain supple-paced :
how little this stark and armoured mouth can say
of the living beast.

THE GREETING

One instant of morning,
he cast a glance
idly, half blindly
into the depths of distance :

space and its Eden
of green and blue
warranted more watching
than such gazing through :

but the far roofs gave
a 'Good day' back,
defeating that negligence
with an unlooked-for greeting :

it was the day's one time
that the light on them
would carry their image
as far as to him

then abandon the row,
its lit-up walls
and unequal pitches,
its sharpness to shadow :

one instant of morning
rendered him time
and opened him space,
one whole without seam.

THE INSISTENCE OF THINGS
paragraphs from a journal

At the edge of conversations, uncompleting all acts of thought,
looms the insistence of things which, waiting on our recognition,
face us with our own death, for they are so completely what we

are not. And thus we go on trying to read them, as if they were signs, or the embodied message of oracles. We remember how Orpheus drew voices from the stones.

It takes so long to become aware of the places we inhabit. Not so much of the historic or geographic facts attaching to them, as of the moment to moment quality of a given room, or of the simple recognitions that could be lured to inhabit a paragraph, a phrase, a snatch of words—and thus speak to us.

A stump of stone juts up out of the grass, glittering drily like weathered cedar. A cloud of gnats dances over it on a now mild December day. It is the remains of a mounting block, disused beside this fenced-off bridge. The gnats haunt the stone as if it held warmth, grey against grey. One can scarcely make out what they are, and their winter dance seems such a weightless celebration of improbables (how did they escape last night's frost?—the birds of the day before?) that what one actually sees is more than the sight—an instance radiating unlooked-for instances, a swarm of unreasoning hopes suddenly and vulnerably brought into the open.

Snow keeps trying the currents of the air—a haze, a smoke of crystals—but each time it is about to take solid shape, the wind whirls it apart into specks of white dust, just visible on the blackness of the surrounding woodland. The thin cry of an early lamb is brought in on the blustering wind that crashes endlessly against the trees. There is an almost metallic edge to that frail voice with which a new energy has entered among the leafless branches, the sudden sun gashes in dark cloud and lancings of green over shallow grass where the rays emerge.

Beech leaves on a small beech, crowded and protected by the closeness of an ill-kept wood. For all the storms, they are still firmly anchored and look like brittle, even fragments of brown paper, their veining very clear and regular. The wind in them hisses faintly, a distinct and crisper hiss than that of the water which fills the distances. The coming and going breaths of the wind: hiss, silence, hiss. The pale brown of the leaves seems among the dark branches to attract light into these scalloped and cupped handshapes.

30

Towards the end of a warm spring day, the evening air, echoing with bird-calls, prepares for frost. A distant half moon in its halo. No cloud near it, only down low on the western horizon where it lies shapeless, thick and pink-purple, more like a mist. In the east, a few feathery drifters also catching the pink, last flare. The map on the moon is visible. A sound as clearly isolated as the moon (a shut door) breaks off from the farm building. The thin cry of lambs, a discussion of rooks above the wood, the insistence of bird-calls. The sound of a farm van winds away through the mingled callings. The rooks are flying round and round in the twilight over the wood, like dirty sediment rising and falling in the water of the air. They argue (or agree?—which?) on one concerted note. A sudden intervention from two wild ducks. An owl takes up the broken note of the ducks, rounds it, mellows it, hollows it to a scream, hoarsely answering a second owl in a new dialogue. As the daylight disappears, the moon casts pallid shadows.

IV HEBRIDEAN PIECES

IDRIGILL

Roofless, the wreck of a house and byre
   Lies like a stone boat, the tide
Behind, inching, ebbing. A high
   Sea could almost float it out
Across that plain of water, to where
   Those who abandoned it still try
To account for their lives here
   Levelled too long, too soon :
Working the waves, they gather up salt sheaves
   That, collapsing, break their hold and spread
In abysses of candour, scatterings of fools' gold.
   That boat would take them in,
Beach them by sea-caves where they might lie
   And face out the storms in sea-cleansed effigy,
If grass had not matted its decks and clasped them down
   To a tranquil earth its owners could never own.

OF LADY GRANGE

Of Lady Grange
        that ill-starred daughter
        of Chiesly of Dalry : he
        who when the Lord President
        sat in adverse judgement
        murdered him :

She inherited
        the violence of her father, was married
        some say against her will, others
        so that she might spy on him
        to Erskine, my Lord Grange,
        Jacobite, profligate and bigot :

He
        and the family she bore him
        detested her : but when a separation

was arranged, my Lady Grange went on
molesting him, opposed as she was
to his politics and his person :

One night—
       it was a decade and more
       after the rebellion and its failure—
       her husband and his friends
       gathered, each to rehearse his part
       in the restoration of the house of Stuart :

The lives
       of men of great family
       were at stake when she, concealed
       it is said beneath a sofa
       or a day-bed where they sat,
       burst forth and threatened to betray them :

James Erskine
       judging her capable of that,
       two gentlemen (attended)
       called at her lodging : her resistance
       cost her two teeth as they forced her
       first into a sedan, then on to horse :

Her husband
       had it given out that she
       was sick of a fever : the next day
       she 'died' of it and he
       saw to it that her funeral should
       have all of the ceremony due to blood :

Her journey
       was as cold as the earth
       her coffin lay in :
       air, spray and the spread of water
       awaited the living woman
       her stone mocked greyly :

They rode
       from Edinburgh to Stirling and despite
       storms, robbers, Highland
       tracks and the lack of them,

reached the deserted Castle Tirrim
at Moidart loch :

Thence
    on by boat, and out
    into the Atlantic : Heiskir
    was to house her two years,
    until the single family there
    could no longer tolerate her

And said so :
    from a ship, two men
    appeared and carried her
    on board to Kilda, where
    no one could speak her language,
    nor would she learn theirs :

She learned
    to spin and in a clew
    of yarn sent with her neighbours' wool
    to Inverness, she hid a message,
    though she had neither pen nor pencil :
    this was the sixth year of her exile :

To Hope,
    her misnamed lawyer,
    the letter seemed
    to be written in blood : a ship
    chartered, fitted and sent
    found without its tenant

The house
    on Kilda, chimneyless, earth-floored :
    for her, once more
    the inevitable sea, Skye
    at last and the sand of a sea-cave
    where fish-nets hung to dry

At Idrigill :
    nor could this place
    keep the secret long :
    though the cliffs hung sheer,

the fishers came
to cure their catch and to sleep here :

Again
      she must be moved on
      and over to Uist : a large
      boulder, knotted in a noose,
      lay in the boat : a guard stood
      ready to sink his charge

If
      rounding a headland of the cliff
      the ship, sighting them,
      should pursue : out into the surge
      oars drew them where
      the three wrecked women

Emerge
      from the sea in stone :
      they were set for the further isles :
      Bracadale sank down
      behind them into its mist :
      now they could only trust

Time
      to weary what vigilance
      might try, and time
      so ruffled and so smoothed
      the sea-lanes they went by,
      was it from Uist, Harris or Assynt

That she
      came back to Skye?
      Of the life she had
      in Vaternish, all we hear
      is of the madness of her last
      and fifteenth year

In exile,
      of 'the poor, strange lady
      who came ashore
      and died', and of the great
      funeral which the Macleod
      of Ramsay's portrait, paid for :

38

Yet still
       no ordinary end
       attended that lonely woman :
       'for reasons unknown'
       the coffin at Duirinish
       held stones only :

But there
       where Kilconan church
       still points at variable skies
       a roofless gable, the square
       stone of a later year
       confesses her corpse :

She
       is well buried above that sea,
       the older dead beside her
       murdered in the burning church
       and, below, their slayers on the same
       day slain, the dyke-wall toppled to cover them.

THE PROMISE

The tide goes down, uncovering its gifts :
   Rocks glint with the silver of slivered wood,
Like the piecemeal skeleton of some great boat,
   That this light of resurrection, if it could
Would draw together again, and the next tide find
   As solid as the cliff that looms behind
Its absence now. But part of a scene
   That is flawed and flowing, the pieces lie
Under a fragmented rainbow's promise
   Of the changes in their unbroken sufficiency.

MARINE

The water, wind-impelled, advancing
   Along the promontory side, continually
Shaves off into spray, where its flank
   Grazes against rock, each white
In-coming rush like a vast
   Wheel spun to nothing, a wing
Caught down from flight to feathers.

RUBH AN' DUNAIN
(The Point of the Forts)

Mouthings of water at the end of a world.
Pictish masons have outreached their enemy
In stone. But who won, or what gods
Saved the bare appearances of it all
Is written in no history.
Their pantheon was less powerful than this wall.

COUPLET

Light catches the sudden metal of the streams :
Their granite captive is stirring in its chains.

V WORDS AND MUSIC

BEETHOVEN ATTENDS THE C MINOR SEMINAR

That was the day they invited
Ludmilla Quatsch, the queen of the sleevenote.
Her works cannot be quoted
Without permission. I shall not quote.

Think and drink were to be paid for
Out of the Gabbocca Fund.
Her theme was 'Arguing About Music'. Her arguments
Had driven T. Melvin Quatsch into the ground.

She challenged Beethoven on the Heiliger Dankgesang :
Too long. Too long. She argued
For a C Minor without final chords
And a Hymn to Joy without the words.

Ah, if only he were here in spirit to agree !
(She knew that she had him confuted)
And suddenly, inexplicably there he was—
Some confusion of levels in the celestial computer

Had earthed him. It was the briefest of appearances,
But up out of vagueness wavering
He seemed to savour her points, and she
Clutched for his attention, all cadenzas and fortissimi.

She had sensed at once the urgency of the event,
Packed-in and pressure-cooked her argument :
By now, the laity were quite lost
As she pitched her apophthegms at that height, that ghost.

He seemed to grow very deaf, and then
(After a slight cybernetic adjustment overhead)
Very dead and disappeared.
Had all she was saying gone unheard?

She thought she still could descry him—
He of the impregnable ear, still quick
To catch only the most hidden sound :
His silence was as unanswerable as his music.

Doubt diminished her. They helped her out.
After which those sleevenotes were never the same
(Too complicated, as I have said, to quote)
—Rumour insisted it was another hand from which they came.

When they invited Ludmilla, all had hoped
That she might return to fill the chair,
But that untimely vision balked
Them and her of twenty years of talk.

CONSOLATIONS FOR DOUBLE BASS

You lament your lot at the bottom of an abyss
    Of moonlight. And yet you would not
Change it for all that bland redundance
    Overhead, the great theme leaping
Chromatic steeps in savage ease.
    The trumpets on their fugal stair
Climb each other's summits pair by pair :
    A memorial of remissive drums. The hero falls.
A race of disappointed generals, we mourn him
    Nobilmente. Confluence of a hundred streams
In one lambency of sound, our grief
    Beckons the full orchestra, 'Come on—
Crash in like a house collapsing
    On top of its hardware.' And you ?
All that you can do is state, repeat,
    For repetition is the condition for remembering
What must come—the moment
    For the return to earth, to blood-beat.
Good gut, resonant belly,
    You are the foot a hundred others
Tread by, the bound of their flying islands
    And their utopias of sound. Tristan is being sung to
Like a drowsy suckling : you
    Are sanchoing still : that, I know,
Is the story of another hero—but you have ridden

44

With them all to their distress, and lived
To punctuate it, unastounded in your endless
Unthanked *Hundesleben*, nose to ground.

MELODY
Song is being . . . *Rilke*

That phrase in the head—that snatch repeated
Could have led nowhere, but for the will
To hear the consequence of it—the reply
To 'I am dying, I am denying, I, I . . .'
A shred of the self, an unease : its pleasure
Would not please the hearer long who heard it
Only within : a violin carries it
To surrounding air, letting it meet
That first and silent pressure, come
To test its setting out, its hovering
Over a spun doubt, its own questioning.
Through a second instrument it flows,
But a third goes counter to it, and a fourth
Derides both the pride and pains
It has taken to stay proud; and forces,
Frees it to a singing strength
Until that thread of song, defied,
Gathering a tributary power, must find
The river course, winding in which
It can outgo itself—can lose
Not the reality of pain, but that sense
Of sequestration : the myth of no future
And no ancestry save ache. *Gesang
Ist Dasein?* Song is the measure, rather,
Of being's spread and height, the moonrise
That tips and touches, recovering from the night
The lost hill-lines, the sleeping prospects :
It is the will to exchange the graph of pain
Acknowledged, charted and repeated, for the range

Of an unpredicted terrain. Each phrase
Now follows the undulations of slope, rise
And drop, released along generous contours
And curving towards a sea where
The play of light across the dark immensity,
Moves in a shimmering completeness. The tide
Ridden in unexulting quiet, rides
Up against the craft that sails it
Tossed and tried, through the groundswell
To the dense calm of unfathomable silence.

DA CAPO

And so
they go back : violin
against piano
to know once more
what it was
they had felt before :

But reapproaching
all they knew
though they touch (almost)
they cannot encroach there :
to know what they knew
and, knowing, seize it,
how should time grow and how
should they reappraise it ?

Time beyond all repeal,
they know that they must feel
now what they know,
and going back
to unenterable Eden, they
enter a time new-made
da capo